this
journal
belongs
to _____

date _____

She believes

that God knows her better
than anyone else ever has
or ever will, so she learns
to trust Him more and more...
with less and less hesitation.

God is greater than our worried hearts and knows
more about us than we do ourselves. 1 John 3:20 MSG

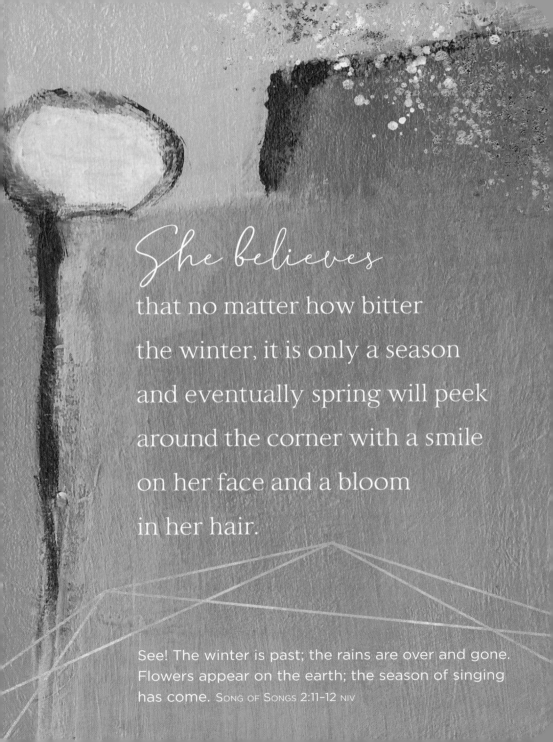

She believes

that no matter how bitter
the winter, it is only a season
and eventually spring will peek
around the corner with a smile
on her face and a bloom
in her hair.

See! The winter is past; the rains are over and gone.
Flowers appear on the earth; the season of singing
has come. Song of Songs 2:11–12 NIV

She believes

there is courage and freedom

in giving every fear and every care

to God because she is His

and He is more than enough.

So humble yourselves under the mighty power of God,
and at the right time he will lift you up in honor. Give all
your worries and cares to God, for he cares about you.
1 PETER 5:6–7 NLT

She believes

that silence often speaks louder

than a thousand voices; and in that

quietness, she learns to listen.

She learns when to speak

and when to keep still.

She learns how to *be*.

In quietness and confidence shall be your strength.
ISAIAH 30:15 NKJV

She believes

that when days of hope

become seasons of holding on,

God is taking the time

to make her story

a beautiful handwritten

script of grace.

I am looking up to You in constant hope.
PSALM 86:3 TLB

She believes

that she's an ordinary girl

chosen by an extraordinary God,

and that every day she's

becoming wholly beautiful

in the wholeness of Him.

Let petitions and praises shape your worries into prayers, letting God know your concerns. Before you know it, a sense of God's wholeness, everything coming together for good, will come and settle you down. Philippians 4:6–7 MSG

She believes

that God can speak

through anything He chooses—

a friend, a stranger, a circumstance.

He is everywhere, always speaking

to those who are willing to listen.

My sheep hear My voice, and I know them, and they follow Me. JOHN 10:27 NKJV

She believes

she is loved unconditionally.
Even with scars, insecurities,
and doubts, still nothing wins
against the power of God's love,
and nothing keeps her
from believing His love
reveals how beautiful
she truly is.

Neither death nor life, neither angels nor demons, neither our fears for today nor our worries about tomorrow—not even the powers of hell can separate us from God's love. ROMANS 8:38 NLT

She believes

all of nature is the voice of God

saying, "I made this for you.

When you feel the wind,

it's my Spirit kissing yours.

When you step out into the rain,

it's my love refreshing your soul."

For since the creation of the world God's invisible
qualities—his eternal power and divine nature—have been
clearly seen, being understood from what has been made.
ROMANS 1:20 NIV

She believes

the storms of life will give way

to a joyful end and a transformed

heart—a heart saturated

with faith in the One

who sees her as priceless.

Everyone can see that the glorious
power within must be from God and
is not our own.... We are perplexed
because we don't know why things
happen as they do, but we don't give
up and quit. 2 Corinthians 4:7-8 TLB

She believes

in the beauty of grace
and the love that comes
from a heart that's been
broken and put back together
by the gentle hands
of a loving God.

He has sent Me to heal the brokenhearted....
To give them beauty for ashes...that He may
be glorified. Isaiah 61:1, 3 NKJV

She believes

that even when the journey
is hard, the road is paved
with grace that keeps her going.

We're not giving up. How could we! Even though on the outside it often looks like things are falling apart on us, on the inside, where God is making a new life, not a day goes by without His unfolding grace. 2 Corinthians 4:16 MSG

She believes

in joy. Not the fleeting
happiness that comes
and goes with the wind,
but the deep-down confidence
that anchors her heart
in the storm.

Let all who take refuge in you be glad;
let them ever sing for joy. Spread your
protection over them, that those who love
your name may rejoice in you. Psalm 5:11 NIV

She believes

God sees her tears when
they fall and collects each one
in an alabaster jar, saving them
to strengthen her soul.
When the time comes,
He'll pour on the courage
she needs to carry on.

You have collected all my tears and preserved them in
your bottle! You have recorded every one in your book.
The very day I call for help, the tide of battle turns....
This one thing I *know: God is for me!* Psalm 56:8–9 TLB

She believes

that forgiveness is the

magical balm that melts away

the rust of bitterness

and opens the door

to healing, peace, and joy.

Oh, what joy for those whose disobedience
is forgiven, whose sin is put out of sight!
Psalm 32:1 NLT

She believes

that it's okay to cry

until her eyes swell

and her nose gets stuffy

and her soul is washed free

of the world's weight...

so her spirit can soar again.

Learn the unforced rhythms of grace. I won't lay anything heavy or ill-fitting on you. Keep company with Me and you'll learn to live freely and lightly. MATTHEW 11:30 MSG

She believes

in the power of a song.
She knows that her Savior
sings over her in a voice
more beautiful than anyone
can imagine.

He will rejoice over you with gladness, He will quiet
you with His love, He will rejoice over you with singing.
Zephaniah 3:17 nkjv

She believes

a broken heart becomes a way
for God's love to break
the dependence she's had
on anyone but Him. Learning
to lean on His strength makes
the days ahead of her sweeter
than they've ever been.

My spirit may grow weak, but God remains the strength
of my heart; He is mine forever. PSALM 73:26 NLT

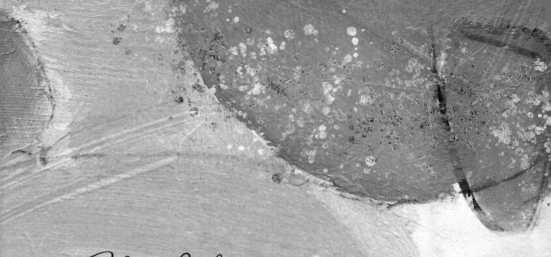

She believes

her moments have God's attention—
and she's becoming more confident
in His faithfulness every day.

Faith is the confidence in what we hope for and the
assurance about what we do not see. HEBREWS 11:1 NIV

She believes

she can live every day

in anticipation of what God's doing

in her life—in all the places

she can't yet see, for all the reasons

she doesn't yet know, to unveil

the dreams she hasn't yet

told anyone but Him.

Look, and be amazed! You will be astounded at what I am about to do! For I am going to do something in your own lifetime that you will have to see to believe. HABAKKUK 1:5 TLB

Ellie Claire
Hachette Book Group
1290 Avenue of the Americas, New York, NY 10104
ellieclaire.com

First Edition: February 2020

Ellie Claire is a division of Hachette Book Group, Inc. The Ellie Claire name and logo are trademarks
of Hachette Book Group, Inc.

Print book interior design by Melissa Reagan.

ISBN: 9781546014515 (softcover)

Printed in China

RRD

10 9 8 7 6 5 4 3 2 1